OCS Study
MMS 2007-030

Coastal Marine Institute

Incorporation of Gulf of Mexico Benthic Survey Data into the Ocean Biogeographic Information System

```
132TT4455A       LONGHORN     STO0011974120319741206J.S. HOLLAND      UNIV. T
132TT4455B0001 281200N 962700W197412052030   OTB     25
132TT4455F0001      100      6177020101       3
132TT4455F0001      100      3760040101       3
132TT4455F0001      100      6189010302     142
132TT4455F0001      100      5105040401       1
132TT4455F0001      100      6186020201       1
132TT4455F0001      100      6177010102       1
132TT4455F0001      100      6177010103      57
132TT4455F0001      100      6186030102       1
132TT4455F0001      100      6189010601       4
132TT4455F0001      100      3758             4
132TT4455F0001      100      6177010402     113
132TT4455F0001      100      6191010101      55
132TT4455F0001      100      6177010202     122
132TT4455F0001      100      6177010701       1
132TT4455T0001      100      STATION:   101  TIME:     SAMPLE ID:  AFL
132TT4455B0002 281200N 962700W197412060915   OTB     25
132TT4455F0002      200      6177020101    2100
132TT4455F0002      200      61791401         1
132TT4455F0002      200      6189010302       5
132TT4455F0002      200      5105040401       1
132TT4455F0002      200      6177010102       1
132TT4455F0002      200      6177010103      28
132TT4455F0002      200      6189010601       5
132TT4455F0002      200      3758             6
132TT4455F0002      200      6177010402       6
132TT4455F0002      200      6191010101      15
132TT4455F0002      200      6177010202      12
```

U.S. Department of the Interior
Minerals Management Service
Gulf of Mexico OCS Region

Cooperative Agreement
Coastal Marine Institute
Louisiana State University

OCS Study
MMS 2007-030

Coastal Marine Institute

Incorporation of Gulf of Mexico Benthic Survey Data into the Ocean Biogeographic Information System

Author

Robert S. Carney

December 2007

Prepared under MMS Contract
1435-01-04-CA-32806-36185
Louisiana State University
Coastal Ecology Institute
Energy, Coast, and Environment Bldg.
Baton Rouge, Louisiana 70803

Published by

U.S. Department of the Interior
Minerals Management Service
Gulf of Mexico OCS Region

Cooperative Agreement
Coastal Marine Institute
Louisiana State University

DISCLAIMER

REPORT AVAILABILITY

Extra copies of the report may be obtained from the Public Information Office (Mail Stop 5034) at the following address:

U.S. Department of the Interior
> Minerals Management Service
> Gulf of Mexico OCS Region
> Public Information Office (MS 5034)
> 1201 Elmwood Park Boulevard
> New Orleans, Louisiana 70123-2394

> Telephone Number: (504) 736-2519
> 1-800-200-GULF

CITATION

Suggested citation:

Carney, R.S. 2007. Incorporation of Gulf of Mexico benthic survey data into the Ocean Biogeographic Information System. U.S. Dept. of the Interior, Minerals Management Service, Gulf of Mexico OCS, New Orleans Region, La. OCS Study MMS 2007-030. 21pp.

SUMMARY

The Minerals Management Service has been one of the primary sources of oceanographic data since it first began supporting offshore sampling of the biota and environment. It has been a stipulation in all such studies that data be filed with the National Oceanographic Data Center (NODC) of the National Oceanic and Atmospheric Administration (NOAA). In addition voucher specimens of all species collected are to be deposited with a repository museum, usually the U.S. National Museum of Natural History. Over the past 10 years there has be a greatly increased interest in the biological diversity of the seafloor. Making use of informatics, scientists are actively re-examining older studies in the search for ecological patterns. The information on benthic community distributions supported by museum specimens comprise one of the best data sources for the study of seafloor ecology available anywhere in the world.

NODC is noted for its exceptional work with archived physical and chemical data, but it lags behind other archiving programs with respect to biological survey data. Innovation in this area lies primarily in the academic and museum communities. The Ocean Biogeographic Information System (OBIS) is under development in the U.S. both as a primary repository of data and a gateway to fully integrated databases elsewhere in the world. Therefore, to assure that MMS-collected data be available for continued analysis, it must be transferred from discontinued NODC formats into OBIS format while there is still some understanding of the older data content.

This project has been a trial effort at carrying out transfer from four Gulf of Mexico data sources: the published results of deep sampling by W.E. Pequegnat, contractor's data archives for the Northern Gulf of Mexico Continental Shelf study, NODC archives of the South Texas OCS study, and NODC archives of the Southwest Florida Benthic Community study. Entry, proofing, and reformatting of the published results proved to be the easiest undertaking. Conversion of all archived data was seriously hampered by the lack of available documentation for the NODC Species Code that has been discontinued. Once Species Code information was finally located, conversion of the NODC MULDARS format required a great deal of manual intervention due to inconsistent use of format standards. Unfortunately, this inconsistency makes it impractical to reformat all data sets with a single computer program. Conversion requires study-by-study custom processing of the data archives.

TABLE OF CONTENTS

LIST OF FIGURES

LIST OF TABLES

1. Introduction

1.1. Intent

The intent of this project is to begin transfer of Minerals Management Service (MMS) legacy data on the distribution of benthic species from archival formats to data elements in a format suitable for modern database analysis, increasingly termed "bioinformatics" (Costello and Berghe 2006). As a trial effort four datasets have been submitted to the Ocean Biological Information System (OBIS). They will be available for study at http://www.iobis.org/. The data type selected for the initial transfer was benthic invertebrates since these studies have been a major component of the comprehensive programs. Four studies were selected for the initial transfer: the South Texas Outer Continental Shelf study (STOCS), the Southwest Florida Shelf Ecosystem study (SWFL), the deep benthic surveys of Willis Pequegnat (PEQ), and the Northern Gulf of Mexico Continental Slope study (NGMCS). The two deep studies were selected due to an increased interest in continental margin ecosystems. The two shelf studies were selected as representative of other MMS surveys in similar habitats. All four studies have available final reports and archived data as hardcopy in appendices to final or interim reports.

The four datasets represent the full range of archival data and associated problems that anyone attempting transfer may encounter. STOCS archives are in relatively good shape and easily obtained. SWFL are in similarly good shape, but were more of a challenge to locate. NGMCS archive files are incomplete requiring that data be mined from hardcopy reports and checked for error by the original contractor. The oldest data, PEQ, predated common use of digital records and could only be obtained from a hardcopy report.

1.2. Content of Report

This report is intended to serve two purposes. First, it details project activity as required by contract. Second, it contains elements of a "users manual" that can aid in the transfer of MMS and other archival datasets describing the distribution of marine species. The report contains a brief discussion of how benthic data are used to serve as guide in deciding what data should be transferred. Old formats, especially those used by the National Oceanographic Data Center (NODC) are discussed along with the emerging OBIS into which the old data are translated. The fact that old formats are fixed while new formats are changing is an important factor in deciding upon a transfer strategy and method. The step-by-step transfer is then detailed for the STOCS dataset and summarized for the others. In discussion, the structure and activity of a larger data transfer effort are outlined. Lastly, conclusions are drawn.

1.3. Management and Scientific Uses of Bioinformatics

While the task of converting old species-level data is a time-consuming effort, it promises to provide both management and science the opportunity to make much greater use of existing information. Bioinformatics as exemplified by OBIS is a growing collection of data and tools that are not fundamentally different in result than traditional analytical approaches in benthic ecology. Prior to the 1960's benthic ecologists carried out quantitative sampling, characterized benthic communities by indicator species, and mapped out species and community distributions (Thorson 1957). As ecological theory advanced and computing power increased there was a shift to understanding causes of distribution, multivariate analyses, and estimating the species diversity of benthic systems (Sanders 1968). This analytical form of benthic ecology was quickly tailored to test for environmental impacts (Green 1979). In reaching results, benthic ecologists have always used georeferenced data, purposeful sampling designs, along with statistical and graphical analyses. New data have always been interpreted in the light of prior knowledge found in the literature about species biology and similar habitats.

The intent of bioinformatics is to make the task of finding patterns in species-level data vastly simpler. In doing so, bioinformatics will allow questions to be explored which would have previously been impractical. For examples, previous studies can be reanalyzed to gain insight for optimal design of new studies. Many sources of original data can be combined for new regional and long-term syntheses. And, older data can be examined using contemporary analyses that may prove more insightful.

The purpose of transferring old archival data to a more modern format is to assure the utility of the data in answering management and scientific questions. Three management needs can be anticipated.

- Review and Re-analysis of Completed Studies – At present, it is impractical to review the results of previous studies at the level of actual data. Bioinformatics will make this highly feasible. Strengths and weaknesses of previous studies will be easily reconsidered.

- Improved Design of New Studies – At present, it is impractical to carry out power analyses of old data to determine the efficacy of proposed sampling designs. Bioinformatics will allow any person planning a benthic survey to fully consider design and results of prior studies in order to arrive at the most cost effective approach.

- Long-term and Cumulative Effects Studies – At present, it is impractical for MMS to fully use the results of old baseline studies to fully test the possibility that offshore development has uniquely impacted local and regional ecologies. Bioinformatics will allow for strong designs that test for both temporal and larger-scale effects.

The scientific use of MMS survey data is somewhat more difficult to predict. Diversity and distribution research, however, have both become extremely active areas of renewed research. Researchers in these areas are actively seeking data sets that will allow new ideas about both to be tested. The MMS-supported baseline data have the potential of being extremely valuable raw material for these studies. Three uses of MMS benthic data can be anticipated on the basis of recent research.

- Applicability of Competing Null Models – Gray et al. (2006) have reconsidered the topic of abundance distributions in the benthos in light of Hubbell's (2001) hypotheses that random effects dominate community abundances. The distributions found in numerous habitats will be actively investigated.
- Effective Measurement of Diversity over Mixed Scales – Grassle and Maciolek (1992) using MMS data attempted to extrapolate diversity from small scale samples to the global scale using what are now considered incorrect assumptions. Considerable progress in the analysis of diversity over scales including extrapolation

has been made (Colwell et al. 2004), and these new techniques will be widely applied to existing data sets.

- Measurement of Taxonomic Diversity – Recently there has been a major departure from traditional measurement of diversity using species richness and abundance. Phylogenetic relationships within community components are now considered an important aspect of diversity measurement (Harper and Hawksworth 1994). Warwick and Clarke (2001) have introduced a suite of such indices that are increasingly applied to benthic systems. The MMS species-level data is an excellent source for the study of these novel diversity measures.

2. MMS and OBIS Benthic Data Archiving

2.1. Traditional MMS Data Archiving

The benchmark and topically-focused studies undertaken by MMS have been a major source of comprehensive oceanographic data since the 1970's (Avent, 2000). Recognizing the long-term value of data, MMS contracts have required submission of all data to NODC and the submission of voucher specimens of collected species to the U.S. National Museum of Natural History or other appropriate repository.

With respect to physical, chemical, and geological data, the NODC and its sister agency the National Geophysical Data Center (NGDC) have effectively carried out and even expanded their role as archivists. Quality controlled data products of great importance in contemporary oceanography include the World Ocean Atlas and the ETOPO2 global bathymetry database. The NODC has been an effective archivist of species survey data, pioneering coding of taxonomic information, but no syntheses have been undertaken or useful data products provided to encourage use. The unfortunate consequence is the development of a reputation for "data in, no data out" among benthic ecologists.

It is obvious from consideration of the components of an analysis that the NODC archives are difficult to use and often incomplete. The main difficulty stems from the fact that information is very difficult to pull together. The detail about stations stored with faunal data are limited to position, sometimes depth, dates, times, and type of sampling gear. Finding a-biotic data requires locating and examining other files in entirely different formats. Similarly, no additional information about the biology of the species are contained within the archive. Finding such taxa-specific information requires converting a numerical code into a species name and then searching the literature. Most critically, no information about sampling design is included in the archives. Such information may be preserved in reports and publication, but if often presented so generally that the analyses can not be duplicated.

2.2. OBIS and Converging Data Standards

Currently there is widespread interest in developing databases to support a range of species-level ecological studies collectively called "biodiversity research." The OBIS is just a single example of this interest that is being put in place by a combination of oceanographic and systematic investigators in the academic sector. The decision as to what MMS should do with survey data needs to take into consideration the overall picture of database development. The major developments are sketched out in this section. MULDARS is the format of pre 1995 data but is no longer supported or required by NODC. The ITIS is an active species-based database that has assumed assignment of taxa codes as initiated by NODC. The FGDC Biological Profile is a metadata standard required for geospatial data such as oceanographic surveys. The Darwin Core is a database growing out of museum curation capable of supporting biodiversity research. OBIS is a modification of the Darwin Core.

2.2.1. MULDARS Format

The MMS data submitted to NODC from 1970 to 1995 are archived in MULDARS (MULti-Discipline Archives Retrieval System) format files. Since 1995, NODC has accepted faunal data in a unrestricted range of formats only requiring that the contents be adequately explained in accompanying metadata. Adequacy of metadata rather than actual data files is assured through adherence to The Federal Geographic Data Committee (FGDC) and the USGS Biological Resources Division (BRD) Biological Profile for metadata.

The MULDARS is based upon the stacks of punched paper cards prevalent in the 1960's – 1970's for input of data. Efficient use of space on the card's 80 columns lead to standard practices of mixing cards with different types of data to prevent redundancy and of using space-saving data formats that required special read formats to parse. Originated specifically for oceanographic data, MULDARS had the capacity to record most information of interest. Unfortunately, no tools were ever developed by NODC for analysis of faunal data in MULDARS format, and the format's archival capacity was never fully utilized.

An extremely important aspect of the MULDARS codes for biological data is that a 12 digit numerical code was used for each taxon rather than a spelled-out name. The NODC based this code on one initiated at Virginia Institute of Marine Science. Use of the codes allowed datasets to omit the longer genus and species names and directly supported analyses requiring numerical values. The function of maintaining the taxonomic code base was passed to ITIS.

2.2.2. The ITIS (Integrated Taxonomic Information System)

The MMS benthic survey data are species-level information that needs to comply with Integrated Taxonomic Information System (ITIS) data standards and benefit from the provided analysis tools. The ITIS is the U.S. Government's response to broad interest in "biodiversity." The ITIS was established in the mid 1990's to coordinate and advance species-level data (http://www.itis.gov/). The ITIS resides in the department of agriculture. The ITIS has supplanted NODC as lead agency in the digital coding of species. The ITIS provides tools for taxonomic data management but has limited analytical capacity at this time. Internationally, ITIS participates in the Global Biodiversity Information System (GBIS, http://www.gbif.org/), a 47 nation collaboration headquartered in Denmark. The GBIS was initiated in 1999 and has links to many more data archives than ITIS. The U.S. participation in GBIS is supported by the National Science Foundation (NSF).

From the perspective of utility in the analysis of MMSD benthic data, ITIS is extremely important with respect to some information about species, but the database does not support ecological or biogeographic analysis directly. The ITIS provides the user two important functions. Details as to use of the system may be found in ITIS (1996).

- It provides a Taxonomic Serial Number (TSN) for all species in the database, greatly simplifying the coding of species names in a database.

- It provides a search engine to international databases and the scientific literature when given a taxonomic name or TSN.

Unfortunately, ITIS is only useful if a species already exists in its database. Addition of a species to the database requires providing as many as 45 data elements and is best left experienced taxonomic experts. Many taxa in MMS studies are not currently in the database, and updating the database would be a major task.

2.2.3. The FGDC (Federal Geographic Data Committee) Biological Profile

The MMS benthic survey data is inherently geospatial in nature and needs to be compliant with the Federal Geographic Data Committee (FGDC) and the USGS Biological Resources Division (BRD) data standard (FGDC and USGS-BRD, 1999). Intended for a great variety of biological data types, this data standard has approximately 80 possible elements. Some provide information on the geospatial location of a species, some information on the exact taxonomic identification, some methodology, and many other elements are used to provide information on the data structure itself. The need to accommodate many different data types generated by many federal programs makes the Biological Profile potentially very complicated to use.

The NODC is a participant in the FGDC and maintains new metadata in general compliance with that standard. The full geospatial and taxonomic detail of the Biological Profile is not, however, required. The data contributor is largely left to submit data using any set of data elements so long as those elements are fully explained at the time of submission. This approach makes data submission much easier but completely ignores the need to make data easily accessible through the use of a standard format. At this time, neither NODC nor FGDC make tools available for access and analysis of data. The current utility of these government efforts for the analysis of MMS benthic surveys is minimal.

2.2.4. OBIS and the Darwin Core

While government database standards tend to be developed by archivist, there are programs outside of government much more oriented to the users of data such as taxonomists, curators, biogeographers, and biological oceanographers. The Darwin Core is a database standard developed and supported by International Working Group on Taxonomic Databases (TDWG) affiliated with the International Union of Biological Sciences (IUBS). In 1994 it broadened its scope from plants to encompass animals, microbes, and fossils. Supported by the Global Biodiversity Information Facility (GBIF) headquartered in Denmark, the Darwin Core has some status as a non-governmental standard. The Darwin Core is strongly internet oriented and uses web development tools to assure openness across participating databases.

The Ocean Biogeographic Information System (OBIS) or International OBIS (IOBIS, www.iobis.org) differs from ITIS, and GBIS in that it is intended to be a tool for ecological study at the species level specifically focuses upon ocean environments. The archival of highest quality species-level data is a necessary first step, but the overall purpose is the understanding of patterns. In effect, OBIS is assuming the role of archivist and analysts for marine biota data that NODC has never fulfilled. The OBIS is headquartered at Rutgers University. It was initiated via the National Ocean Partnership Program (NOPP) in 2000. Support is primarily through the Census of Marine Life Program of the A.P. Sloan Foundation.

5

3. Conversion Task

The worked reported here had two subtasks. The first was to develop a procedure and methods for data conversion from MULDARS to OBIS format. The second was to apply these to four faunal surveys supported by MMS.

3.1. Conversion Procedure

Obtaining NODC archives as 2004 was a slow process requiring correspondence with a data specialist and the preparation by NODC of a data tape or uploading ftp files (file transfer protocol site) for retrieval. Getting the correct files sometimes required repeated attempts since the search routines used by the archivists were prone to error. Presently, most of the old archives are accessible online via the Ocean Archive System at http://www.nodc.noaa.gov/cgi-bin/search/prod/accessionsView.pl/prefs. There is, however, no supporting metadata.

Locating correct files via the on-line search, requires repeated attempts searching with different criteria. The experience of this project was that searches using information recorded on the "A" record were most effective. This includes the research vessel name, the principal investigator, and the collecting organization. Searches on data type, specifically benthic species, produced incomplete data location. Similarly, searches on project titles such as Southwest Florida Shelf Ecosystem Study located only a portion of the available data. Confirmation that the located data were actually from the targeted project had to be based upon reading of the final report and determination of the dates and coordinates of sampling.

3.2. Data Elements Available from NODC in MULDARS Format

The MULDARS code for data archiving was used by NODC from 1970 to 1995. Its convention of using different types of records to store several data elements and requiring FORTRAN formats to access the values have greatly reduced the formats utility in a modern computing environment. A knowledge of this format and common deviations from it's full implementation are vital to any task of archive conversion. Full format and explanations are still available online at the time of this report (http://www.nodc.noaa.gov/General/NODC-datafmts.html).

Benthic fauna data employ MULDAR F132 format with up to 7 different types of records combined into a single file. Each record is a "card image" in the sense having 80 characters. Data are recorded as ASCII characters in fields of precise position and lengths. To save space, there are no delimiters between data elements and decimal points are omitted. Breaks between data elements and the position of decimals within numbers were intended to be controlled by FORTRAN format read statements at the time of analysis.

The structure of a F132 file strongly reflects the nature of benthic fauna surveying in the late 1960's. Datasets were primarily identified by research ship, cruise designation, and dates. This information along with an investigator name and institution were recorded at the beginning of each data file using an "A" record format.(Figure 3.1). Each file contains only a single "A" record. It is the first line or record in the file. Preceding the "A" character are information signifying that the data is in F132 format and the name given the file in the NODC archive. In some instances file have become concatenated during the archiving process and more than one "A" card may exist in a file.

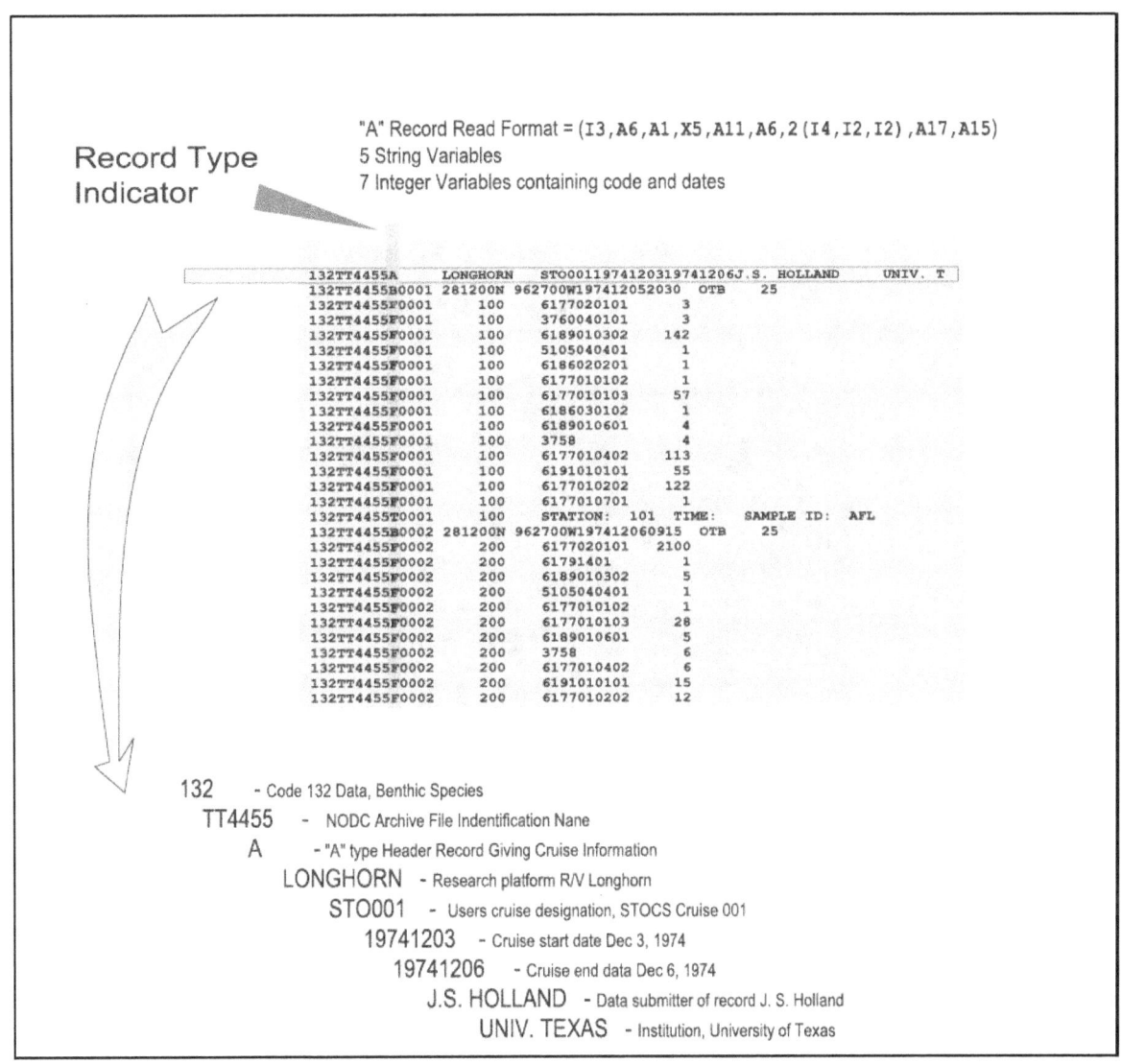

Figure 3.1. Each file has a single "A" card giving study and cruise information.

Secondary identification of data was based upon geospatial station coordinates, dates, and a code for sampling activity. The F132 format recognized two types of sampling method, towed devices like trawls ("B" record format) and fixed point devices ("C" record format). The placement in a file of these records are shown in Figures 3.2 and 3.3 respectively. Each file will contain as many samples as there are for the cruise specified on the "A" record. A non-standard feature found in many files is that a "B" and "C" record are included for each sample even though only one sampler was used. This greatly complicates the task of determining which gear was used. Usually, however, the species caught in trawl samples are distinct from those commonly collected in box cores and grabs. This allows the determination to be correctly made but requires sample-by-sample examination of the file. A peculiarity of the F132 format is the difference between data elements for towed devices ("B" format) and coring devices ("C" format). Both records have fields that can be used to record some aspects of the equipment and sample processing. Only "B" records, however, include depth. In order to include this critical element in a reformatted file, it's necessary to locate depth data in the printed reports, if they can be found there.

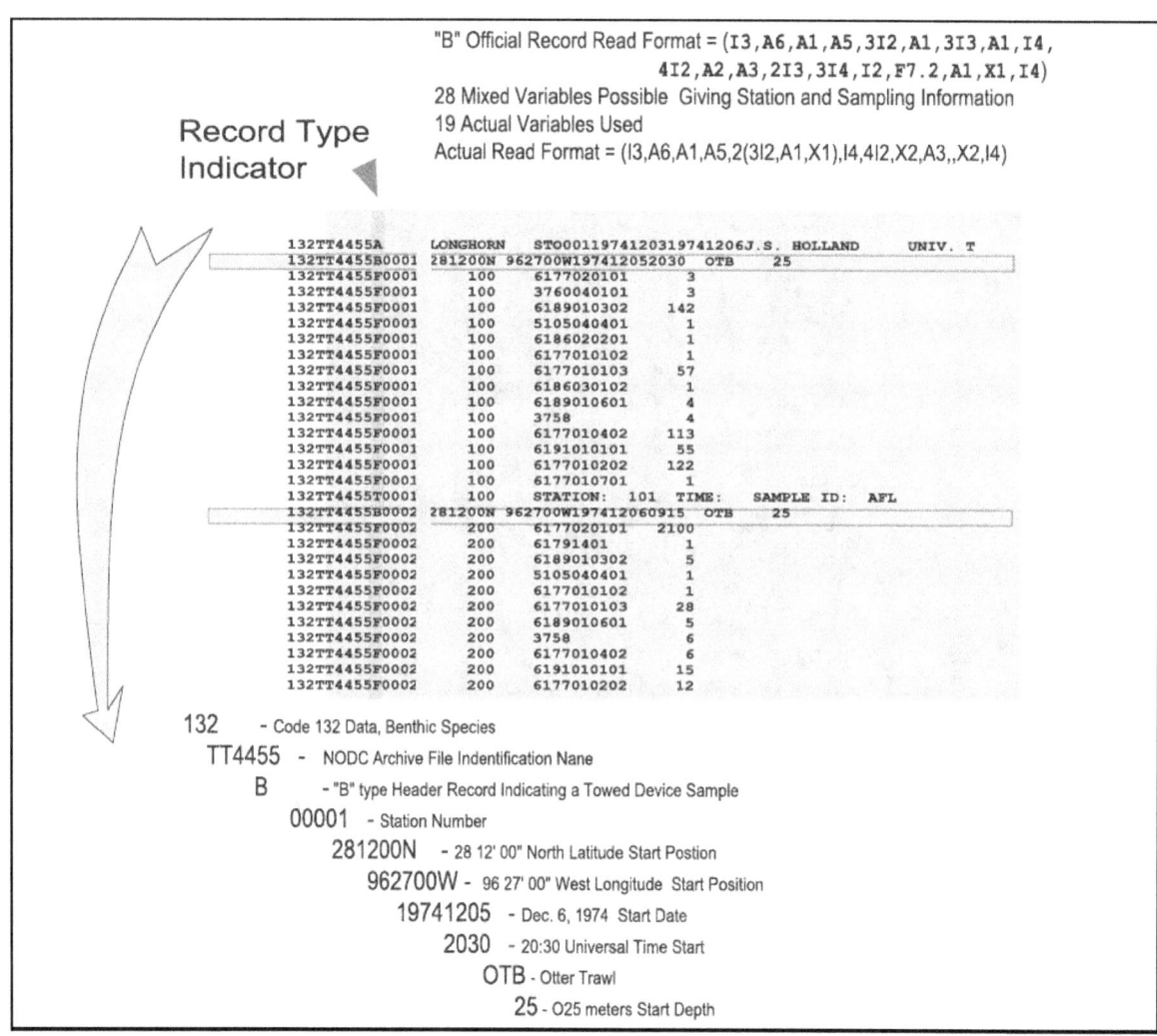

Figure 3.2. Each sample taken with a towed device has a "B" record giving station information.

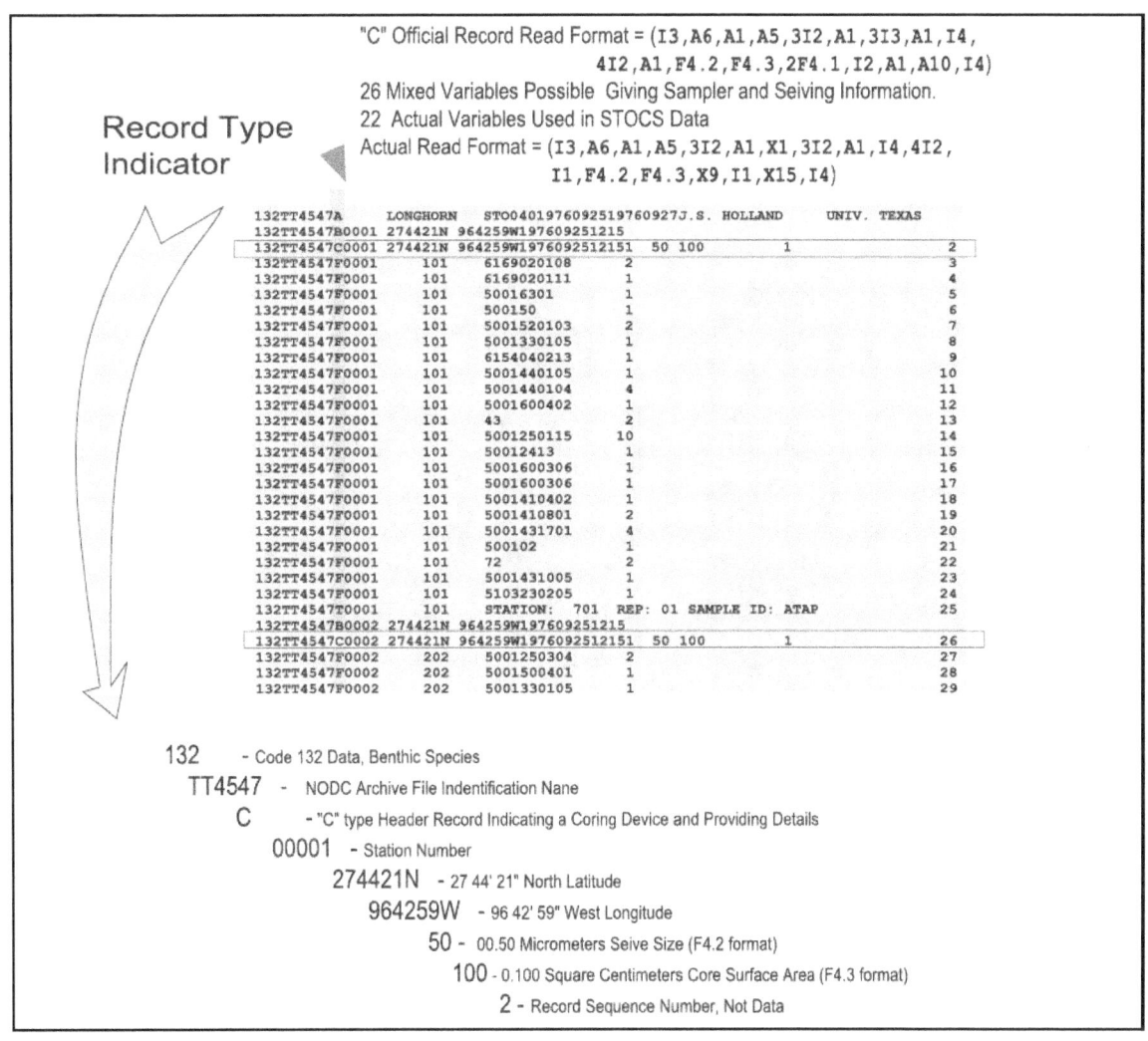

Figure 3.3. Each sample using a core or grab has a "C" record giving station information.

Sample information given on the "B" or "C" record can be augmented with addition of an "D" and "E" record for surface and bottom conditions respectively. None of the datasets reviewed in this project made use of these auxiliary records. The only practical method of finding parallel data on chemistry, temperature, or sediment properties is to determine if they exist by reading project reports. Subsequently, a search for appropriate files in the NODC archive can be conducted. Each data type employs a distinctly different MULDARS format.

Following all the cruise, sample, and environmental records is a sequence of faunal data records using the "F" format in which a taxonomic code, count, weight, and a limited amount of specimen derived data can be entered (Figure 3.4). Most records in a file consist of these "F" records. There can be inconsistency as to how counts and biomass are represented. The values may be either raw counts or densities expressed per unit area. To the data user, the only means of confidently determining exactly what the data represent is to compare the archives with the narrative provided in project reports.

9

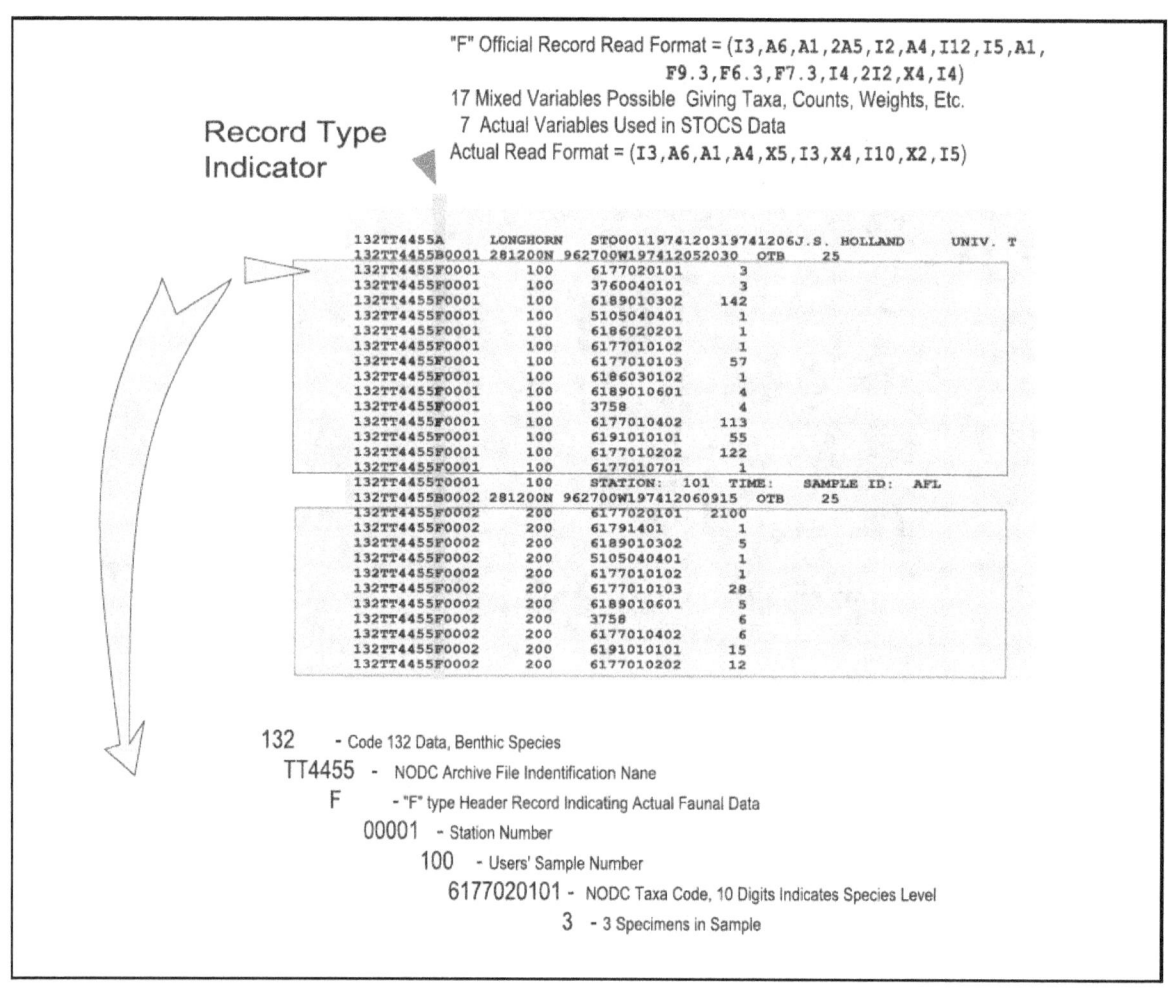

"F" Official Record Read Format = (I3,A6,A1,2A5,I2,A4,I12,I5,A1,
F9.3,F6.3,F7.3,I4,2I2,X4,I4)
17 Mixed Variables Possible Giving Taxa, Counts, Weights, Etc.
7 Actual Variables Used in STOCS Data
Actual Read Format = (I3,A6,A1,A4,X5,I3,X4,I10,X2,I5)

Record Type Indicator

```
132TT4455A       LONGHORN      STO0011974120319741206J.S. HOLLAND      UNIV. T
132TT4455B0001 281200N 962700W197412052030 OTB      25
132TT4455F0001      100      6177020101      3
132TT4455F0001      100      3760040101      3
132TT4455F0001      100      6189010302    142
132TT4455F0001      100      5105040401      1
132TT4455F0001      100      6186020201      1
132TT4455F0001      100      6177010102      1
132TT4455F0001      100      6177010103     57
132TT4455F0001      100      6186030102      1
132TT4455F0001      100      6189010601      4
132TT4455F0001      100      3758            4
132TT4455F0001      100      6177010402    113
132TT4455F0001      100      6191010101     55
132TT4455F0001      100      6177010202    122
132TT4455F0001      100      6177010701      1
132TT4455T0001      100      STATION:   101   TIME:   SAMPLE ID:  AFL
132TT4455B0002 281200N 962700W197412060915 OTB      25
132TT4455F0002      200      6177020101   2100
132TT4455F0002      200      61791401        1
132TT4455F0002      200      6189010302      5
132TT4455F0002      200      5105040401      1
132TT4455F0002      200      6177010102      1
132TT4455F0002      200      6177010103     28
132TT4455F0002      200      6189010601      5
132TT4455F0002      200      3758            6
132TT4455F0002      200      6177010402      6
132TT4455F0002      200      6191010101     15
132TT4455F0002      200      6177010202     12
```

132   - Code 132 Data, Benthic Species

TT4455 - NODC Archive File Indentification Nane

F   - "F" type Header Record Indicating Actual Faunal Data

00001 - Station Number

100 - Users' Sample Number

6177020101 - NODC Taxa Code, 10 Digits Indicates Species Level

3 - 3 Specimens in Sample

Figure 3.4.   Faunal counts or biomass are recorded on "F" records that follow the "B" or "C" sample records.

A final record type encountered in the F132 files is a "T" (text) record (Figure 3.5). These may be inserted any place in the file that the investigator feels the need for additional information. There is no standardization of usage. In the STOCS study they were used to indicate the end of a sample and to give an alternative station identifier.

Conceptually, MULDARS-to-OBIS conversion should be a simple programming task. The geospatial, time, date, and sampling information contained on "A," "B," and "C" records must be read and then added to the data on each "F" record to produce a new record suitable for OBIS. Unfortunately, there are so many inconsistencies and errors in format usage that the task becomes much more complex. Among problems encountered are that. whole "B" and "C" records are sometimes missing. This has the effect of incorrectly pooling two or more samples. Within the same study the F132 strict column placement of data may be violated between and within files. This causes serious misreads potentially making a count of 100 either a 10 or a

10

1000. Species codes sometime are entered in the position reserved for counts with the result of exceptionally high counts.

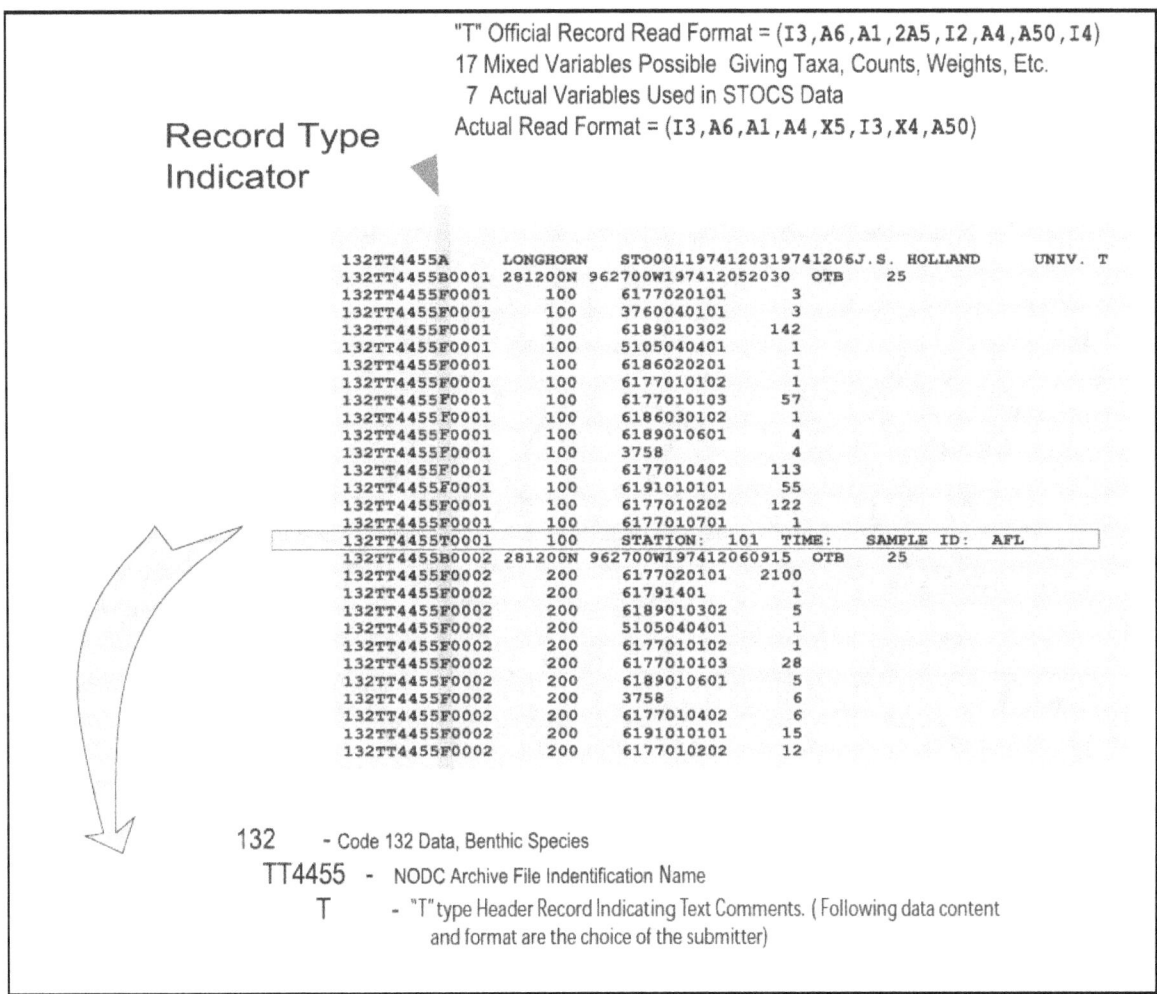

Figure 3.5. Text or "T" records can be placed anywhere in file giving any information the investigator considers important.

3.3. Data Elements Required by OBIS

Where MULDARS is a very compact and almost cryptic format, OBIS can be very detailed and redundant but easily understood. The OBIS schema is a modification of the Darwin Core explained above. With a background in collection management, OBIS has features associated more with taxonomy than oceanography. There are currently 73 data elements in OBIS, but only 7 are absolutely required: species name, latitude, longitude, and four elements primarily associated with database management. Fortunately, those 7 required elements can either be directly obtained from F132 records or easily developed from project reports. Even in this limited form, the OBIS files could be used to determine species distributions or fauna within specified geographic regions.

11

The correspondence between data elements in the OBIS and MULDARS F132 systems are shown in Table 3.1. For this project the decision was made to provide 27 OBIS data elements in all cases and to provide 7 additional taxonomic elements when possible. These are presented in Table 3.1. Of 70 possible elements in OBIS, only 14 are directly available from the MULDARS format files. Additional elements, however, can be developed from project reports and museum collections.

Table 3.1.
Data Element Correspondence between OBIS and MULDARS F132

Number	Data Element Name	Required	Available from MULDARS F132 Archives	Method of F132 – OBIS Conversion
1	Date Last Modified	Y	N	Must be created during conversion
2	Institution Code	Y	N	Enter as "NODC/MMS" for MMS-derived data at NODC
3	Collection Code	Y	Y	NODC Track Number cols. 4 – 9 on all records
4	Catalog Number	Y	N	Museum Catalog Number if specimens are archived. Otherwise, "null"
5	Record URL	N	N	http//:www.nodc.noaa.gov.
6	Scientific Name	Y		NODC records contain numerical codes that are no longer supported. A look-up table must be constructed and used.
7	Basis of Record	N	N	"O" for observation, code most suitable for MMS fauna data
8	Source	N	N	"R.S. Carney" or any person converting and submitting data
9	Citation	N	N	Open literature publication for the study if possible. Otherwise Final Report
10	Kingdom	N	N	"Animal"
11	Phylum	N	N	Can be derived from NODC Taxonomic Code or ITIS look up.
12	Class	N	N	Can be derived from NODC Taxonomic Code or ITIS look up.
13	Order	N	N	Can be derived from NODC Taxonomic Code or ITIS look up.
14	Family	N	N	Can be derived from NODC Taxonomic Code or ITIS look up.
15	Genus	N	N	Can be derived from NODC Taxonomic Code or ITIS look up.
16	Subgenus	N	N	Can be derived from NODC Taxonomic Code or ITIS look up.
17	Species	N	N	Can be derived from NODC Taxonomic Code or ITIS look up.
18	Subspecies	N	N	Can be derived from NODC Taxonomic Code or ITIS look up.
19	Name Author	N	N	Can be derived from ITIS look up.
20	Identified By	N	N	Possibly available in final report, but listed expert may have only seen voucher specimens and the actual ID made by unknown person.

Table 3.1. Data Element Correspondence between OBIS and MULDARS F132 (continued)

Number	Data Element Name	Required	Available from MULDARS F132 Archives	Method of F132 – OBIS Conversion
21	Year Identified	N	N	Generally not available information unless data can be linked to a museum voucher specimen.
22	Month Identified	N	N	Generally not available information unless data can be linked to a museum voucher specimen.
23	Day Identified	N	N	Generally not available information unless data can be linked to a museum voucher specimen.
24	Type Status	N	N	Refers only to specimens in museums. Use that institutions designation.
25	Collector's Number	N	N	Generally not available information. Collector's inventory system for field samples.
26	Field Number	N	Y	Station code should be in cols 11-15 on B and C records
27	Collector	N	Y	In cols 49-66 on A records
28	Year Collected	N	Y	In cols 31-34 on B and C records
29	Month Collected	N	Y	In cols 35-36 on B and C records
30	Day Collected	N	Y	In cols 37-38 on B and C records
31	Start Year Collected	N	N	For long-time observations, not applicable to typical survey
32	Start Month Collected	N	N	For long-time observations, not applicable to typical survey
33	Start Day Collected	N	N	For long-time observations, not applicable to typical survey
34	End Year Collected	N	N	For long-time observations, not applicable to typical survey
35	End Month Collected	N	N	For long-time observations, not applicable to typical survey
36	End Day Collected	N	N	For long-time observations, not applicable to typical survey
37	Julian Day	N	N	Must be calculated
38	Start Julian Day	N	N	For long-time observations, not applicable to typical survey
39	End Julian Day	N	N	For long-time observations, not applicable to typical survey
40	Time of Day	N	N	In cols 39-42 B and C records as hours and minutes converted to decimal hours
41	Start Time of Day	N	N	For long-time observations, not applicable to typical survey
42	End Time of Day	N	N	For long-time observations, not applicable to typical survey
43	Time Zone	N	N	Assume to be local time but varies with vessel operator.
44	Continent or Ocean	N	N	OBIS referenced URL for Master Directory of names of bodies of water no longer exists. "Gulf of Mexico" used in this project

Table 3.1. Data Element Correspondence between OBIS and MULDARS F132 (continued)

Number	Data Element Name	Required	Available from MULDARS F132 Archives	Method of F132 – OBIS Conversion
45	Country	N	N	"USA" if applicable
46	State or Province	N	N	"Texas," "Louisiana," Etc. as applicable
47	County	N	N	Not applicable
48	Locality	N	N	Might be in final report for special reefs, banks, etc.
49	Longitude	Y	Y	Cols 23-28 on D and C records. Must be Converted from deg, min, sec to decimal degrees.
50	Start Longitude	N	N	Not available, only start, duration, course, and time on B record
51	End Longitude	N	N	Not available, only start, duration, course, and time on B record
52	Latitude	Y	Y	Cols 16-21 B and C records. Must be converted from deg, min, sec to decimal degrees.
53	Start Latitude	N	N	Not available, only start, duration, course, and time on B record
54	End Latitude	N	N	Not available, only start, duration, course, and time on B record
55	Coordinate Precision	N	N	"NULL" Information may be available in final report, but some studies used nominal coordinates for stations with multiple samples rather than actual fixes.
56	Start/End Precision	N	N	"NULL" Information may be available in final report, but some studies used nominal coordinates for stations with multiple samples rather than actual fixes.
57	Bounding Box	N	N	Not well explained in OBIS schema
58	Minimum Elevation	N	N/Y	Depth of collection as negative meters. Cols 54-57 on B records only. For C records must be developed from final report.
59	Maximum Elevation	N	N/Y	Depth of collection as negative meters. Cols 54-57 on B records only. For C records must be developed from final report.
60	Minimum Depth	N	N/Y	Depth of collection as positive meters. Cols 54-57 on B records only. For Records must be developed from final report.
61	Maximum Depth	N	N/Y	Depth of collection as positive meters. Cols 54-57 on B records only. For C records must be developed from final report.
62	Depth Range	N	N	Not applicable for F132 files. Used for older literature where only a distribution range is used.
63	Temperature	N	N	In cols 33-37 of E records if available
64	Sex	N	N	Seldom included for survey data.

Number	Data Element Name	Required	Available from MULDARS F132 Archives	Method of F132 – OBIS Conversion
65	Life Stage	N	N	Seldom included for survey data.
66	Preparation Type	N	N	Applicable only for voucher collection
67	Individual Count	N	N	Applicable only for voucher collection
68	Observed Count	N	Y	In cols 39-43 F record
69	Observed Weight	N	Y	Wet weight in cols 45-53 of F record if used. Ash-free weight in cols 54-59 of F record if used. Convert from grams to kilograms OBIS fails to specify which weight is preferred
70	Previous Catalog Number	N	N	Relates to changes of database through time. Not applicable at this time.
71	Relationship Type	N	N	Applicable when organism associations exists such as epizoa, symbiote, etc. Possibly available in final report
72	Related Catalog Item	N	N	Applicable when organism associations exists such as epizoa, symbiote, etc. Possibly available in final report
73	Notes	N	Y	Contents of T records

3.4. OBIS Data Elements to be Developed from Outside NODC Archives

Based on the review of data element correspondence it was judged feasible to develop a subset of 38 shown in Table 3.2. Of these 12 dealing with taxonomic details are considered optional and should be added in the future during taxonomic review. The impracticality of adding full taxonomic information stems from the lack of such information for many marine species in the ITIS system that has replaced the NODC species codes. Ideally, faunal records could be linked to U.S. National Museum of Natural History catalogue numbers. Unfortunately, the USNM system can not support such a link at this time.

From the perspective of MMS and scientists carrying out benthic surveys, OBIS is not a sufficient data archive. There are two serious omissions. First, there is no means of recording critical information about sampling methods other than to use Notes (Data Element 70). Second, there is no means of indicating the intended design of sampling except to use an *ad hoc* scheme of station and sample coding. These shortcomings of OBIS illustrate how important it is to provide as much detail as possible in final reports and to continue the filing of archival data with NODC.

Actual OBIS files ready for submission are delimited text files. Each data element must be in correct sequence and separated by a text character agreed upon with the OBIS staff. Comma delimited files were created in this study. The step-by-step process of conversion is detailed in Section 5.

Table 3.2.
Restricted OBIS Data Elements Developed during Conversion

Number	Data Element Name	Method of F132 – OBIS Conversion
1	Date Last Modified	Must be created during conversion
2	Institution Code	Enter as "NODC/MMS" for MMS-derived data at NODC
3	Collection Code	NODC Track Number cols 4-9 on all records
4	Catalog Number	Museum Catalog Number if specimens are archived. Otherwise, "null"
5	Record URL	http://www.nodc.noaa.gov
6	Scientific Name	NODC records contain numerical codes that are no longer Supported. A look-up table must be constructed and used.
7	Basis of Record	"O" for observation, code most suitable for MMS fauna data
8	Source	"R.S. Carney" or any person converting and submitting data
9	Citation	Open literature publication if possible. Otherwise Final Report
10	Kingdom	"Animalia"
11	Phylum	Can be derived from NODC Taxonomic Code or ITIS look up.
12	Class	Can be derived from NODC Taxonomic Code or ITIS look up.
13	Order	Can be derived from NODC Taxonomic Code or ITIS look up.
14	Family	Can be derived from NODC Taxonomic Code or ITIS look up.
15	Genus	Can be derived from NODC Taxonomic Code or ITIS look up.
16	Subgenus	Can be derived from NODC Taxonomic Code or ITIS look up.
17	Species	Can be derived from NODC Taxonomic Code or ITIS look up.
18	Subspecies	Can be derived from NODC Taxonomic Code or ITIS look up.
19	Name Author	Can be derived from ITIS look up.
20	Identified By	Possibly available in final report, but listed expert may have only seen voucher specimens and actual ID made by unknown person.
26	Field Number	Station code should be in cols 11–15 on B and C records
27	Collector	In cols 49-66 on A records
28	Year Collected	In cols 31-34 on B and C records
29	Month Collected	In cols 35-36 on B and C records
30	Day Collected	In cols 37-38 on B and C records
40	Time of Day	In cols 39-42 B and C records converted to decimal hours
43	Time Zone	Assume to be local time but varies with vessel operator.
44	Continent or Ocean	OBIS referenced URL for Master Directory of names of bodies of water no longer exists. "Gulf of Mexico" used in this project
45	Country	"USA" if applicable
46	State of Province	"Texas," "Louisiana," Etc. as applicable
48	Locality	Might be in final report for special reefs, banks, etc.
49	Longitude	Cols 23-28 on D and C records. Converted to decimal degrees.
52	Latitude	Cols 16 -21 B and C records. Converted to decimal degrees.
55	Coordinate Precision	"NULL" Information may be available in final report, but some Studies used nominal coordinates for stations with multiple samples rather than actual fixes.
61	Maximum Depth	Depth of collection as positive meters. Cols 54-57 on B records only. For C records must be developed from final report.
68	Observed Count	In cols 39-43 F record
69	Observed Weight	Wet weight in cols 45-53 of F record if used. Ash-free weight in cols 54-59 of F record if used. Convert from grams to kilograms. OBIS fails to specify which weight is preferred.
70	Notes	Contents of T records (if any) and NODC Codes

3.5. Conversion Experience from Four Studies

The STOCS benthic data set was located by means on an online search of the NODC archive. Searching sought files using the Contributing Project option set to "OCS So Texas" and produced 11 accessioned data sets. Descriptions of contents were not very informative, so all sets were opened and examined. Benthic fauna files were located in accession number 8500179. The URL is http://www.nodc.noaa.gov/archive/arc0001/8500179/02-version/data/0-data/recovered/F132-Benthic_Organisms/. Hardcopy data are archived in appendix G of the final report (University of Texas Marine Science Institute 1977).

The downloaded folder contained 145 separate files. The "A" records in all files was read, and it was quickly determined that there were two problems at the file level. First, the OCS So Texas dataset also contained 36 misplaced files from the MAFLA project. Second, the critical fixed format of F132 records was violated slightly in the actual STOCS files and more irregularly for the misplaced MAFLA files. These obvious format errors necessitated file-by-file error checking and format repair.

Review of 109 STOCS files found 79 to contain species-level identification and 30 a lower taxonomic resolution meiofauna study attributed to W.E. Pequegnat. The 79 species-level files contained 51,278 lines of data, enough to fill ~900 printed pages in MULDARS F132 format. There were 870 unique taxa codes and 58 unique station codes. Of all the records, 44,963 contained faunal information. Readily detectable errors were found on 201 records (0.447% error) which lacked species codes completely but contained both count data and a record sequence number. No practical means exists to check for errors of miscoded species or counts.

The search for NGMCS archives was also carried out on line seeking entries associated with the project name. The NODC Archive contained only two F132 files representing only a small part of the project data. Greg Boland of MMS New Orleans was able to obtain data files from LGL Environmental Research Associates and made these available for the conversion process. These files were consistent with EXCEL spreadsheet software and did not require the complex reformatting of MULDARS F132 files. The files were simply augmented with the elements needed to meet OBIS requirements. Data that should have been on "A," "B," and "C" records were developed from the project final report. A hardcopy of full replicate data are contained in Gallaway (1988). Typographical errors, however, do exist in that report. Therefore, the LGL and OBIS databases are the only corrected archive sources.

The PEQ data was converted entirely from hardcopy. The deep Gulf of Mexico sampling of Willis Pequegnat and his associates had never been previously entered in a digital database. The station-by-station data are contained in Pequegnat et al. (1983) in simple text format. These were manually copied into computer files and the OBIS-required elements added. Unfortunately, specimen counts were omitted from the publication.

The experience with the Southwest Florida Ecosystem Study (SWFL) study demonstrated the complexity of dealing with archival data. The SWFL is listed in the NODC archive search function, but a search on that keyword failed to produce benthic F132 data files. Searching on the alternate Gulf of Mexico Southwest Florida Shelf Benthic Communities produced similar negative results. Files were eventually located by searching on the R/V *Sea Venture* used in the study. Use of the NODC archive was complicated by mixed usage of NODC Species Codes and provisional codes created by the investigators. Fortunately, Appendix B of the second year report contains both the codes, species names, and data at the replicate level for the major coring and trawling efforts (Woodward-Clyde Consultants and Continental Shelf Associates 1985).

4. Discussion of Experience and Recommendations

In the course of this project we encountered problems that were both expected and unexpected. A larger-scale conversion of MMS-collected data requires resolution of each of these.

4.1. Data Availability and Quality

The primary lesson learned is that legacy data sets are not uniformly available in archived digital form in spite of MMS' contract requirements. The STOCS and SWFL were found in the NODC archives but were not easily located using the search features provided. The NGMCS archives were incomplete, and the PEQ data never filed. Therefore, the hardcopy data reports submitted in the course of studies are the most reliable source of data. Unfortunately, for the old studies considered here, the digital copies of these reports are scanned images rather than text files. Attempts to extract data using optical character readers were largely unsuccessful due to image quality and blurred typewriter fonts. Manual reading and entry seem to be the most effective means of converting these important data.

When data were submitted to NODC it was often the final task of a project and errors went undetected by the investigators and by NODC staff. Since archived data have seldom been used, errors persist. Catching errors will be difficult unless there are gross omissions that can be found in computer screening of many thousands of records. These gross errors, at least, can be corrected through reference to the project reports. Unfortunately, errors that are in both files and reports can not be corrected. Reanalyzes should always consider the possibility of undetected data errors.

4.2. Critical NODC Taxonomic Code Problem

Completely unexpected and nearly fatal to project success was the finding that the old NODC Taxonomic Code is no longer supported by any archival program in the U.S. Government. The NODC archives in MULDARS format make use of a 12-digit numerical code. When NODC was supporting this code, files necessary for conversion from the code to taxonomic names were available for purchase from NODC. When ITIS assumed the role of taxa coder, a new system of numbering was applied, Taxonomic Serial Numbers (TSN). The NODC issued one final set of conversion files (NODC, 1996) and stopped support. On special request, NODC did provide conversion files for this project, but the CD is no longer publicly available. This means that old files can only be converted by workers able to obtain the conversion files. Without access to the species code, the hardcopy data in reports again become the only useful archive.

4.3. Limited Access to U.S. National Museum of Natural History Catalogue

An extremely important aspect of MMS benthic fauna data is the linkage to museum voucher specimens. Recognizing the great value of voucher-backed data, OBIS included data elements to capture such information. For this project, it had originally been hoped that catalog numbers could be provided linking fauna data with voucher specimens in the U.S. National Museum of Natural History. The Invertebrate Zoology Catalog of the Museum is now online http://goode.si.edu/webnew/pages/nmnh/iz/Query.php. Searching on "MMS" in 2006 yielded an impressive 83,210 records. Searching on "MMS + Gulf of Mexico" produced a similarly impressive 18,203 records. Unfortunately, the intensive interaction with the Museum database needed to search for sample-specific vouchers is not now supported. Hand-entered species by species searching on line followed by station by station comparison is not practical.

18

The U.S. National Museum continues to work with voucher specimens from MMS studies. A future component of such work might be to merge faunal data in OBIS with catalog information. Only the museum staff has sufficient access to records to make this practical.

5. Conclusions and Recommendations as to Conversion

In conclusion it can simply be repeated that MMS-collected benthic data represent an outstanding resource for better management and more informative science. The potential power of informatics is quite impressive. Unfortunately initial hopes that conversion of old archives into the bioinformatic format of OBIS would be a simple computer programming exercise have proven naive. Each easy step of computer conversion must be preceded and followed by careful data checking.

The computer conversions in this task were programmed using a high-level environment, Precision-Visuals Workstation Analysis and Visualization Environment (PV-WAVE). Several similar software packages exist. All that is required is a programming environment that supports the FORTRAN-like read formats required to parse MULDARS format files and to carryout routine manipulation of data strings. Many steps examining the MULDARS files and finishing the final OBIS file can be carried out very effectively with any word processor of spreadsheet software.

The preceding sections have considered the utility of data conversion and looked in detail at data available in NODC archives versus the requirements of OBIS. As a trial effort, this project tried several approaches to data conversion and found some more effective than others. Based on this experience, the following process of conversion is recommended.

1. Value - The MMS, along with interested parties, should review all past studies making the determination as to which datasets have the greatest potential utility to management and to basic research, then obtain all available literature on those projects. Criteria for selection could include the likelihood for long-term study, the quality of the taxonomic information, the habitat sampled, etc.

2. Availability - There are three potential sources of faunal data from MMS projects. The project reports should be considered the primary source if species-level, sample-by-sample data are provided. The NODC archives may exist, and the investigator or contractor may have retained records. All three sources should be checked and as many versions as possible obtained.

3. Obtain F132 files from NODC - conversion of multiple large datasets is only feasible if digital files are available. Hand entry from hardcopy is feasible only in special cases. Locating the necessary file via NODC on-line searches is relatively easy if the vessels used are known.

4. Confirm File Content - Open each NODC archive file in any text editor and confirm from content of all "A" records (platform, date, investigator, and institution) that it is the appropriate study. Project details in the published accouns will allow such confirmation to be made. No special programming is needed.

5. Confirm and Fix Format - Determine the column placement of data in "A," "B," "C," "D,""E," "F," and "T" records and confirm by inspection that the same format is used throughout the entire file. Deviation from specified format is common. If inconsistencies exist for a few records, corrections can be made using a text editor. If inconsistencies exist in a great many records, a program must be written in some string handling language and corrections made or the data discarded.

6. Create OBIS-type Records - Using any string handling language like Basic or higher-level programs like Mat Lab take the data from each F record and combine that with needed geospatial and station information from the preceding A, B, or C records.

7. Convert Taxonomic Codes to Names - Following creation of the initial OBIS-like file from step 6 convert taxonomic codes. If actual NODC Taxonomic Codes were used, and programming language capable of comparing two sets of numbers can be used to make the replacement. If *ad hoc* codes have been used, the reports must be consulted and conversions may species by species using any word processor.

8. Develop Critical Missing Data - The OBIS-like file created in steps 6 and 7 may lack required OBIS data elements. In such a case, the missing information is probably in the hardcopy reports and can be added manually using any word processor or spreadsheet software.

9. Proofing - Line-by-line comparison of many thousands of lines of data is impractical. However, a set percentage of records in the final OBIS file should be manually checked against the hardcopy reports. Ten percent is a minimum number. Simple ecological analyses can also be run looking for improbable results.

10. Develop Metadata -The OBIS requires metadata be submitted with the dataset created in steps 6 through 8. This information can be obtained from the reports and from the database itself. Of special utility are references to MMS reports, museum vouchers, and details about sampling design.

11. Submit to OBIS – Currently, OBIS offers the option of submission of files to reside on an OBIS server. With increasing use of distributed databases across the Internet, however, future submission may consist simply of an address link.

6. Literature Cited

Avent, R. 2000. Minerals Management Service Environmental Studies Program: A history of biological investigations in the Gulf of Mexico, 1973-2000. U.S. Dept. of the Interior, Minerals Management Service, Gulf of Mexico OCS Region, New Orleans. LA. OCS Report MMS 2004-015. 42 pp. Available online at http://www.gomr.mms.gov/homepg/regulate/environ/studies/2004/2004-015.pdf.

Carney, R.S. 1996. On the adequacy and improvement of marine benthic impact surveys: Examples from the Gulf of Mexico outer continental shelf. In: Schmitt, R.J. and C.W.

Osenberg, eds. Detecting ecological impacts: Concepts and applications in coastal habitats: Chapter 15. New York, NY: Academic Press. Pp. 295-216.

Colwell, R.K., C.X. Mao, and J. Chang. 2004. Interpolating, extrapolating and comparing incidence-based species accumulation curves. Ecology 85:2717-2727.

Costello, M.J. and E.V. Berghe. 2006. Ocean biodiversity informatics: A new era in marine biology research and management. Marine Ecology Progress Series 316:203-214.

FGDC Biological Data Working Group, and USGS Biological Resources Division. 1999. Content Standard for Digital Geospatial Metadata - Biological Data Profile, FGDC-STD-001.1.1999. Federal Geographic Data Committee. Washington, D.C. http://www.fgdc. gov/standards/projects/index_html.

Gallaway, B.J., ed. 1988. Northern Gulf of Mexico continental slope study, final report: Year 4. Volume III: Appendices. U.S. Dept. of the Interior, Minerals Management Service, Gulf of Mexico OCS Region, New Orleans, LA. OCS Study MMS 88-0054. 378 pp. Available online at http://www.gomr.mms.gov/PI/PDFImages/ESPIS/3/3697.pdf.

Grassle, J.F. and N.J. Maciolek. 1992. Deep-sea species richness: Regional and local diversity estimates from quantitative bottom samples. American Naturalist 139:313-341.

Gray, J.S., A. Bjørgesæter, K.I. Ugland, and K. Frank. 2006. Are there differences in structure between marine and terrestrial assemblages. Journal of Experimental Marine Biology and Ecology 330:19-26.

Green, R.H. 1979. Sampling design and statistical methods for environmental biologists. New York, NY: John Wiley and Sons, Inc. 257 pp.

Harper, J.L. and D.L. Hawskworth. 1994. Biodiversity: Measurement and estimation, preface. Philosophical Transactions Royal Society London Series B 345:5-12.

Hubbell, S.P. 2001. The unified neutral theory of biodiversity and biogeography. Princeton, NJ: Princeton University Press. 256 pp.

Integrated Taxonomic Information System (ITIS). 1996. Taxonomic workbench users guide version 1.12, October 1996. U.S. Department of Agriculture, Natural Resources Conservation Service, Washington, DC. 46 pp. Available online at http://www.itis.gov/ twb_ug.pdf.

National Oceanographic Data Center (NODC). 1996. NODC taxonomic code, version 8.0 on CD-ROM. (no longer available from NODC).

Pequegnat, W.E, L.H. Pequegnat, J.A. Kleypas, B.A. James, E.A. Kennedy, and G.F. Hubbard. 1983. The ecological communities of the continental slope and adjacent regimes of the northern Gulf of Mexico: Text, photographic atlas, and appendicies. Prepared for the U.S. Dept. of the Interior, Minerals Management Service, New Orleans, LA. Contract #AA851-CT1-12. 696pp. Available online at http://www.gomr.mms.gov/PI/PDFImages/ ESPIS/3/3899.

Sanders, H.L. 1968. Marine benthic diversity: A comparative study. The American Naturalist 102:243-282.

Thorson, G. 1957. Bottom communities. In: Hedgepeth, J.W., ed.. Treatise on Marine Ecology and Paleoecology. The Geological Society of America Memoir 67:461-534.

University of Texas Marine Science Institute. 1977. Environmental studies, south Texas outer continental shelf, biology and chemistry: Final report. Volume IV: Appendix G. Invertebrate epifauna and macroinfauna. Submitted to the U.S. Dept. of the Interior, Bureau of Land Management, Washington, DC. Contract #AA550-CT6-17. 588 pp. Available online at http://www.gomr.mms.gov/PI/PDFImages/ESPIS/3/4075.pdf.

Warwick, R.M. and K.R. Clarke. 2001. Practical measures of marine biodiversity based on relatedness of species. Oceanography and Marine Biology Annual Review 39:207-231.

Woodward-Clyde Consultants and Continental Shelf Associates. 1985. Southwest Florida shelf ecosystem study – Year 2. Volume VI: Appendices. Prepared for the U.S. Dept. of the Interior, Minerals Management Service, New Orleans, LA. Contract No 14-12-0001-29144. 404 pp. Available online http://www.gomr.mms.gov/PI/PDFImages/ESPIS/3/3832.

The Department of the Interior Mission

As the Nation's principal conservation agency, the Department of the Interior has responsibility for most of our nationally owned public lands and natural resources. This includes fostering sound use of our land and water resources; protecting our fish, wildlife, and biological diversity; preserving the environmental and cultural values of our national parks and historical places; and providing for the enjoyment of life through outdoor recreation. The Department assesses our energy and mineral resources and works to ensure that their development is in the best interests of all our people by encouraging stewardship and citizen participation in their care. The Department also has a major responsibility for American Indian reservation communities and for people who live in island territories under U.S. administration.

The Minerals Management Service Mission

As a bureau of the Department of the Interior, the Minerals Management Service's (MMS) primary responsibilities are to manage the mineral resources located on the Nation's Outer Continental Shelf (OCS), collect revenue from the Federal OCS and onshore Federal and Indian lands, and distribute those revenues.

Moreover, in working to meet its responsibilities, the **Offshore Minerals Management Program** administers the OCS competitive leasing program and oversees the safe and environmentally sound exploration and production of our Nation's offshore natural gas, oil and other mineral resources. The MMS **Minerals Revenue Management** meets its responsibilities by ensuring the efficient, timely and accurate collection and disbursement of revenue from mineral leasing and production due to Indian tribes and allottees, States and the U.S. Treasury.

The MMS strives to fulfill its responsibilities through the general guiding principles of: (1) being responsive to the public's concerns and interests by maintaining a dialogue with all potentially affected parties and (2) carrying out its programs with an emphasis on working to enhance the quality of life for all Americans by lending MMS assistance and expertise to economic development and environmental protection.